MOUNTAIN HABITATS

by Alfonso DiBergamo

Harcourt
SCHOOL PUBLISHERS

Cover, p.3, p.5, ©PhotoDisc; p.7, ©Garry Black/Masterfile; p.9, ©Greg Stott/Masterfile; p.11, ©PhotoDisc/PunchStock; p.13, ©Corbis; p.14, ©Pavel Filatov/Alamy.

Cartography, p.4, p.6, p.8, p.10, p.12, Joe LeMonnier

Printed in China

ISBN 10: 0-15-350199-5
ISBN 13: 978-0-15-350199-9

Ordering Options
ISBN 10: 0-15-349939-7 (Grade 4 ELL Collection)
ISBN 13: 978-0-15-349939-5 (Grade 4 ELL Collection)
ISBN 10: 0-15-357282-5 (package of 5)
ISBN 13: 978-0-15-357282-1 (package of 5)

1 2 3 4 5 6 7 8 9 10 985 12 11 10 09 08 07 06

A mountain range is a group of mountains. Mountain ranges can be very long. Some mountain ranges cover thousands of miles. Mountain ranges are also wide. Some of them may be hundreds of miles wide.

There are mountain ranges all over the world on every continent. There are mountain ranges in North America and South America. There are many mountain ranges in Africa, Asia, Europe, and Australia. There is even a mountain range in Antarctica.

The Rocky Mountains

The Rocky Mountains are a large mountain range that is located in North America. The Rocky Mountains stretch from Canada to Mexico. The mountain range is about 3,000 miles (4,828 km) long. The Rocky Mountains cross the western part of the United States.

Many people visit the Rocky Mountains. Some people go there to camp. Other people go there to hike. People also like to fish there. The tops of some of the mountains are always covered with snow. Many people ski down these mountains in the winter.

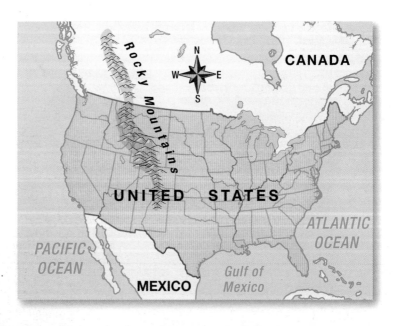

Many kinds of large animals live in the Rocky Mountains. Black bears and grizzly bears live there. Mountain lions live there. Deer, elk, and moose live there, too.

Some of the animals that live in the Rocky Mountains are small. A lot of squirrels and prairie dogs live there. There are also many birds in the Rocky Mountains. Bald eagles, falcons, and owls live there. There are a lot of lakes and rivers in the Rocky Mountains. Fish, frogs, and toads live in those waters.

The Appalachian Mountains

There is another large mountain range in North America. These mountains are called the Appalachian Mountains. The Appalachian Mountains are in the eastern part of North America. They start in Canada. They run for 2,000 miles (3,218 km). The Appalachians end in the state of Alabama.

The Appalachian Mountains are very old. In fact, these mountains are some of the oldest mountains on earth. Some large rivers flow through the Appalachian Mountains. The rivers wash away rocks and soil. This is called erosion. Erosion has formed many deep canyons in the Appalachian Mountains.

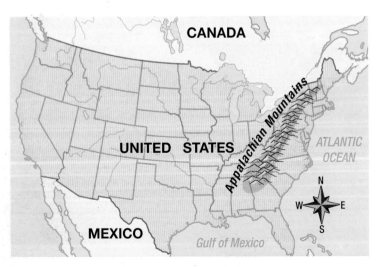

The Appalachian Mountains have many natural resources. Natural resources are materials from the earth that people use. The mountains have a lot of coal. People burn coal for heat. The mountains also have a lot of granite. Granite is a very hard rock. People use granite to make floors and other things. The mountains also have many trees. People cut down the trees for wood. The wood is used to build houses and furniture.

The Andes Mountains

The Andes Mountains are a large mountain range. They are located in the western part of South America. The Andes Mountains run for 5,500 miles (8,851 km). The Andes Mountains begin in the country of Colombia and end in the country of Chile. Chile is located at the very bottom tip of South America.

The Andes Mountains have many volcanoes. One of the volcanoes is named Mount Sangay. It is always erupting. Hot lava constantly comes out of this volcano.

There are many plateaus in the Andes Mountains. A plateau is a wide, flat area of land. The plateaus in the Andes Mountains are high up. The plateaus are usually cold. There is very little rainfall on these plateaus. This makes it hard to grow plants there. People use the land to raise animals instead. People raise cows to get beef. They raise sheep to get wool. They raise goats to get milk.

It is hard to build roads in the Andes Mountains. Many people who live there do not have cars. They use animals such as horses and donkeys to get around instead.

The Alps

There is a large mountain range in Europe called the Alps. The Alps are a very wide mountain range. They are 125 miles (201 km) wide and 750 miles (1,207 km) long.

Thousands of people visit the Alps to ski each year. The Alps are steep and rocky mountains. Many of the mountains are covered with snow all year long. There are about 600 ski resorts in the Alps. A ski resort is like a hotel. People stay in the hotel at night and ski during the day.

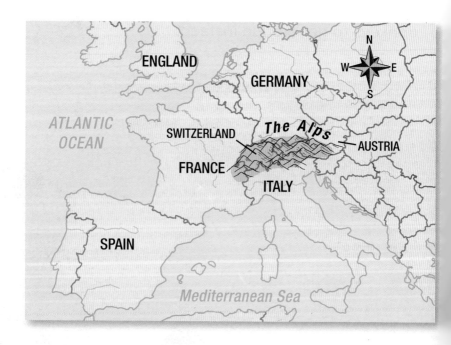

The Alps help form Europe's rivers. First, the snow in the Alps melts, and the water runs down the mountains. Then, small streams of water come together to form creeks. The creeks come together to form a river. The Po River starts in the Alps and flows through the country of Italy.

There are large tunnels in the Alps. A tunnel is a passageway cut through a mountain. People built the tunnels so that cars and trains could travel through the Alps.

The Himalayas

The Himalayas are a large mountain range in Asia. They go through the countries of India, Nepal, Bhutan, Pakistan, and China. The Himalayas are about 1,550 (2,494 km) miles long.

The Himalayas are the highest mountains in the world. The world's highest mountain, Mount Everest, is located in the Himalayas. In fact, nine out of ten of the world's highest mountains are located in the Himalayas.

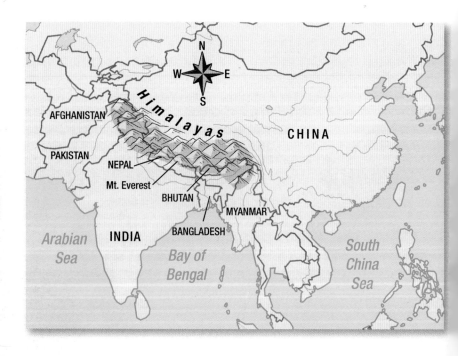

The Himalayas are very steep mountains. The tops of the mountains are jagged, or sharp. The weather is very cold, windy, and snowy on the tops of these mountains.

There are huge glaciers in the Himalayas. Glaciers are large sections of ice that slowly move down the side of a mountain. In the summer, parts of these glaciers melt. The water runs down the mountains and forms large rivers. The huge glaciers in the Himalayas supply water to seven large rivers in Asia.

Other Mountain Ranges

There are other large mountain ranges in the world. The Ural Mountains are the dividing line between Europe and Asia. These mountains run from north to south. The Australian Alps are located in Australia. These mountains have snow on their tops for five to six months each year.

There are mountains all over the world! They provide homes for animals and water for rivers. People enjoy mountain activities and the beauty of the mountains. They are a very important part of our world.

Scaffolded Language Development

SUBJECT-VERB AGREEMENT Review subject-verb agreement with students by modeling for students how to make the subject and the verb agree in number: *A person walks down the street;* and *People walk down the street.* Then read the following sentences, and have students chorally say whether they are "right" or "wrong." If a sentence is wrong, have a volunteer correct the sentence.

1. The Rocky Mountain range <u>stretch</u> from Canada to Mexico.
2. The mountains <u>has</u> many natural resources.
3. The mountains <u>are</u> beautiful in the fall.
4. Every year many people <u>hike</u> the Appalachian Trail.

Have students write a sentence with a singular subject and a sentence with a plural subject.

Science

Mountains of Research Have each student choose a mountain range from the book. Then, using the book and other materials, have students write three descriptive sentences about the mountain range.

School-Home Connection

Mountain Pictures Have students share some of the things they learned about mountain ranges with family members. Then have them talk with family members about mountains they may have seen or read about.

Word Count: 1,019